Family Th In Las Vegas On & Off The Strip

Mini-Adventure Las Vegas Family Travel Guide with Fun-Filled Adventures for Kids and Parents!

Mike Robinson

MW00896819

Copyright © 2024 by Mike Robinson.

All rights reserved. No part of this book may be used or reproduced in any form whatsoever without written permission except in the case of brief quotations in critical articles or reviews.

Printed in the United States of America.

Book design by Mike Robinson
Cover design by Mike Robinson

First Edition: October 2024

CONTENTS

For a unique family dining experience after visiting the Natural History Museum, try Makers & Finders, a vibrant Latin café offering hearty arepas, empanadas, and other dishes that will satisfy adventurous palates. Their diverse kids' menu and fun atmosphere make it a great spot to refuel while introducing children to new flavors... 15

No exploration and discovery adventure is complete without a few creative ways to help your family capture the magic of your journey. Here are some fun ideas to enhance your day out in Las Vegas.. 15

1. Photo Safari Challenge: Equip your kids with disposable or digital cameras and challenge them to take pictures of unique

This chapter of your "Mini-Adventure Planner – Las Vegas, NV-USA Edition" offers a fresh take on Las Vegas, designed to inspire a love of learning and exploration in children while creating

Introduction

Welcome to Las Vegas, a city known for its glitz and glamor, but also filled with countless family-friendly adventures waiting to be discovered! Whether you're visiting for the first time or returning for another unforgettable experience, this guide is crafted to help you and your children explore the very best that Las Vegas has to offer—from thrilling outdoor escapes to fascinating educational trails, and everything in between.

Las Vegas is not just about bright lights and casinos. In fact, for families with children aged 3-15, it's a city packed with unique experiences that will inspire curiosity, creativity, and a sense of wonder. From science museums to outdoor adventures and foodie trails, there's something here for every member of the family to enjoy. Our goal with the *Mini-Adventure Planner – Las Vegas, NV-USA Edition* is to transform your visit into an adventure, encouraging you to make memories that will last a lifetime.

Imagine a city where you can explore prehistoric fossils, get hands-on in science exhibits, hike through beautiful red rock landscapes, and top off the day with a family-friendly dinner at a place that serves delicious food for both picky eaters and adventurous young palates. Las Vegas has it all, and we've mapped out a series of mini-adventures designed with families like yours in mind.

So, get ready for an adventure of a lifetime. In this book, we'll introduce you to new places, give you insider tips for fun activities, and guide you through the exciting culture and history of Las Vegas—ensuring that you leave the city with unforgettable memories.

How to Use This Book

This book is designed to help you plan your family's time in Las Vegas with ease and excitement. We've structured the content into themed chapters, each focusing on different aspects of the city's unique offerings. These mini-adventures are tailor-made for families and crafted to engage children of different ages and interests. Let's break it down:

1. **Adventure Themes**: Each chapter is centered on a theme such as outdoor activities, cultural experiences, creative arts, culinary delights, and educational science trails. These themes are chosen to cater to a variety of interests, allowing families to pick and choose what suits them best on any given day.

2. **Itinerary Suggestions**: Each chapter includes a half-day and full-day itinerary. This flexibility means you can fit these adventures into your schedule, whether you're looking for a quick exploration or planning an all-day event. Feel free to mix and match activities from different chapters to customize your trip!

3. **Detailed Activities**: We've made sure to provide detailed descriptions of every stop on your adventure. This includes essential information like addresses, operating hours, and contact details, so you'll have everything you need at your fingertips. We've also added little-known tips to make your visits smoother and more enjoyable.

4. **Family-Friendly Dining Recommendations**: We know how important it is to find restaurants that everyone in the family can enjoy. For each chapter, you'll find carefully selected dining spots that cater to children's tastes while offering something exciting for parents as well. From themed eateries to places that offer interactive dining experiences, we've got you covered.

5. **Creative Memory Makers**: Our mini-adventures aren't just about visiting places—they're about creating lasting memories. That's why each chapter includes suggestions for creative activities, whether it's starting a family travel journal, participating in a local craft workshop, or taking photos in iconic locations. These prompts help you make the most of your family time together.

6. **Customizable Options**: We recognize that every family is different, so we've included tips on how to customize each adventure to suit your needs. Whether your children are younger and need more breaks or older and ready for a full day of excitement, you'll find suggestions on how to tailor the experience to fit your family.

By using this book as your guide, you'll not only discover new places but also get the tools to make your time in Las Vegas as smooth and memorable as possible. So, get your cameras ready, pack some snacks, and let the adventures begin!

About the City

Las Vegas, often dubbed "The Entertainment Capital of the World," is renowned for its neon lights, world-class shows, and vibrant nightlife. But beneath its flashy exterior lies a rich history and a treasure trove of family-friendly experiences. Founded in 1905, Las Vegas has transformed from a small desert railroad town into a global tourism hub, but its story is far from just about casinos and entertainment.

In the early 20th century, Las Vegas was a crucial stopping point for railroads and was known for its proximity to the Hoover Dam, which remains one of the most impressive engineering marvels in the United States. Families visiting Las Vegas can explore this history through various museums, exhibits, and even tours that take you into the heart of the dam's construction.

Beyond the city's modern attractions, Las Vegas is surrounded by stunning natural landscapes, from the rugged Red Rock Canyon to the towering peaks of Mount Charleston. This juxtaposition of urban energy and natural beauty makes Las Vegas a perfect destination for families looking to combine education and fun. You can spend the morning learning about the stars at a planetarium and the afternoon hiking through rock formations millions of years old.

Another unique aspect of Las Vegas is its deep connection to art and culture. While the city is known for its high-energy performances, it's also home to a vibrant arts scene, particularly in the Downtown Arts District. This area offers families a chance to explore local galleries, attend outdoor art fairs, and even participate in hands-on workshops that foster creativity in children and adults alike.

Fun Fact: Did you know that Las Vegas is home to some of the most iconic neon signs in the world? In fact, these glowing relics of the past are preserved at the Neon Museum, where families can take a nighttime tour to see the signs light up and learn about the history behind them.

With its combination of history, culture, and outdoor beauty, Las Vegas offers families the chance to dive deep into a world of exploration. Every corner of the city has a story to tell, and we're here to help you uncover the best of them.

Additional Information

Before diving into your adventures, here are a few extra tips to make your family trip to Las Vegas even more enjoyable:

1. **Weather Considerations**: Las Vegas is in the desert, so temperatures can get extremely hot, especially in the summer months. Make sure to carry plenty of water, wear sunscreen, and plan outdoor activities for early morning or late afternoon to avoid the midday heat. Conversely, the winters can be surprisingly cool, so bring layers if you're visiting during the cooler months.

2. **Transportation**: While the Las Vegas Strip is very walkable, many family-friendly attractions are a bit off the beaten path. Consider renting a car if you're planning on exploring the nearby national parks or visiting attractions outside of the Strip. Alternatively, Las Vegas offers convenient public transportation options and rideshare services like Uber and Lyft.

3. **Safety Tips**: Las Vegas is a bustling city, and it's important to stay vigilant, especially in crowded areas like the Strip. Keep an eye on your little ones, and make sure they know what to do if they get separated. If you're visiting outdoor areas, familiarize yourself with local wildlife and desert safety guidelines—such as avoiding certain plants and watching for wildlife like snakes.

4. **Make It a Learning Experience**: While Las Vegas is full of fun, it's also a great city for learning. Engage your children by discussing the science behind the neon lights, the history of the Hoover Dam, or the cultural significance of the city's architecture. Encourage them to ask questions and explore the city with a sense of curiosity.

With this guidebook in hand, you and your family are ready to explore the magic and wonder that Las Vegas holds beyond its famous Strip. From science and history to food and outdoor fun, the adventures waiting for you are bound to inspire. Happy exploring!

This introduction sets the stage for an incredible family adventure in Las Vegas, highlighting the city's rich offerings for children and adults alike. Enjoy the ride, and remember, every adventure is what you make of it!

Las Vegas Quotes Page

Here are some memorable and iconic quotes about Las Vegas that capture the city's unique allure and charm. These quotes would be perfect for setting the tone in your guidebook:

1. **"Las Vegas is sort of like how God would do it if he had money."** – Steve Wynn
   Wynn's quote highlights the grandeur and opulence that Las Vegas is known for, making it a perfect way to reflect on the city's extravagant nature.

2. **"What happens in Vegas stays in Vegas."** – Famous Las Vegas Slogan
   Perhaps one of the most famous sayings about the city, this slogan encapsulates the sense of freedom and fun that draws millions of visitors each year.

3. **"Las Vegas looks the way you'd imagine heaven must look at night."** – Chuck Palahniuk
   This quote emphasizes the city's dazzling nighttime skyline, showcasing the glitz and glamour of the neon lights that light up the Strip.

4. **"Vegas means comedy, tragedy, happiness, and sadness all at the same time."** – Artie Lange
   Lange's words reflect the mixed emotions and whirlwind experiences that a city as multifaceted as Las Vegas can evoke.

5. **"For me, Vegas is a vacation from being smart."** – Penn Jillette
    The famous magician offers a lighthearted perspective on the
    escapism that many visitors experience when they come to Las
    Vegas.

6. **"Las Vegas is the only place I know where money really talks –
    it says, 'Goodbye.'"** – Frank Sinatra
    Known for his love of the city, Sinatra humorously captures the
    essence of Vegas as a place of indulgence and spending.

7. **"Las Vegas is not a city but a world unto itself."** – Michele
    Fiore
    This quote sums up the distinctiveness of Las Vegas, highlighting
    how it offers something for everyone.

CHAPTER 1

Adventure 1: Exploration & Discovery

Las Vegas, NV, may be known for its bustling Strip and adult-centered attractions, but there's a world of family-friendly exploration and discovery waiting for those who seek it. This chapter will guide your family on a mini-adventure through the unique, lesser-known corners of Las Vegas, offering experiences that spark curiosity, foster learning, and encourage family bonding. With exciting landmarks, interactive tours, and hidden gems, families with children aged 3 to 15 will discover a side of Las Vegas they never imagined.

Itinerary Overview

This chapter provides both half-day and full-day itineraries that take families through unique exploration and discovery experiences in Las Vegas. Whether you're looking to immerse your family in the natural wonders of the Mojave Desert, learn about ancient civilizations at local museums, or uncover hidden artistic and cultural gems, these itineraries promise an engaging and educational experience.

- **Half-Day Option**: Begin with a morning visit to the **Las Vegas Natural History Museum**, followed by an early lunch at a local family-friendly restaurant. Finish with a visit to the **Springs Preserve**, a lush oasis that offers nature walks and interactive exhibits.

- **Full-Day Option**: After the museum and lunch, continue your exploration with an afternoon at the **Clark County Wetlands Park**, perfect for families who love nature trails and hands-on learning about local wildlife.

Each option balances learning with adventure, leaving room for flexibility and family fun.

Detailed Activities and Experiences

Exploration and discovery take on new life in Las Vegas with these carefully curated activities designed to engage the minds and imaginations of young adventurers.

Las Vegas Natural History Museum

Located just north of the Strip, this museum is a treasure trove for young explorers. Families can journey through time and space by visiting the museum's engaging exhibits, such as the Prehistoric Life Gallery, which features life-sized dinosaurs, or the Marine Life Gallery, showcasing sharks, rays, and other sea creatures. The museum's "Treasures of Egypt" exhibit is particularly captivating, offering an immersive exploration of ancient Egypt, complete with a replica tomb of King Tutankhamun.

- **Address**: 900 Las Vegas Blvd N, Las Vegas, NV 89101
- **Phone**: (702) 384-3466
- **Website**: https://www.lvnhm.org
- **Operating Hours**: Mon-Sun 9:00 AM - 4:00 PM

Springs Preserve

Springs Preserve, a 180-acre cultural and historical landmark, is an absolute must for families seeking to explore the natural side of Las Vegas. With botanical gardens, walking trails, and interactive exhibits on sustainability and desert life, there's something for everyone. Children will love the Origen Museum within the preserve, featuring hands-on exhibits that focus on Nevada's wildlife and ecosystems. Be sure to check out the seasonal Butterfly Habitat, where kids can walk among fluttering butterflies and learn about their lifecycle.

- **Address**: 333 S Valley View Blvd, Las Vegas, NV 89107
- **Phone**: (702) 822-7700
- **Website**: https://www.springspreserve.org
- **Operating Hours**: Daily 9:00 AM - 5:00 PM

Clark County Wetlands Park

For families looking for an off-the-beaten-path nature experience, Clark County Wetlands Park offers a peaceful escape from the city's hustle and bustle. This hidden gem provides easy hiking trails along the Las Vegas Wash, a natural channel that brings water to Lake Mead. The Wetlands Nature Center offers hands-on exhibits about local wildlife, habitats, and conservation efforts. Families can spot birds, insects, and even the occasional turtle while walking the trails, making this a great educational outing for young nature lovers.

- **Address**: 7050 Wetlands Park Ln, Las Vegas, NV 89122
- **Phone**: (702) 455-7522
- **Website**: https://www.clarkcountynv.gov/government/departments/parks__ _recreation/wetlands_park/index.php
- **Operating Hours**: Daily 6:00 AM - Sunset (Nature Center: 9:00 AM - 3:00 PM)

Family-Friendly Dining Recommendations

Las Vegas is known for its diverse culinary scene, and while future chapters will cover this in detail, here are some dining options close to your exploration destinations that are perfect for the family.

Springs Café

Located within the Springs Preserve, Springs Café offers stunning views of the Las Vegas Strip and surrounding valley. This café is the perfect spot for families to relax and recharge during a day of exploration. The menu features a range of kid-friendly favorites, such as sandwiches and salads, while adults can enjoy fresh and locally inspired dishes like artisanal flatbreads and seasonal salads. With its scenic location and convenient setting within one of Las Vegas' most beloved outdoor attractions, Springs Café makes for an excellent family dining choice.

Address: 333 S Valley View Blvd, Las Vegas, NV 89107
Phone: (702) 822-7700
Website: https://www.springspreserve.org/visitor-information/cafe.html

Makers & Finders

For a unique family dining experience after visiting the Natural History Museum, try Makers & Finders, a vibrant Latin café offering hearty arepas, empanadas, and other dishes that will satisfy adventurous palates. Their diverse kids' menu and fun atmosphere make it a great spot to refuel while introducing children to new flavors.

- **Address**: 1120 S Main St #110, Las Vegas, NV 89104
- **Phone**: (702) 586-8255
- **Website**: https://www.makerslv.com

Creative Memory Makers

No exploration and discovery adventure is complete without a few creative ways to help your family capture the magic of your journey. Here are some fun ideas to enhance your day out in Las Vegas.

1. **Photo Safari Challenge**: Equip your kids with disposable or digital cameras and challenge them to take pictures of unique plants, animals, or landmarks they discover during their outings at Springs Preserve or Wetlands Park. Award prizes for the most creative shots or the rarest finds.
2. **Adventure Journals**: Bring along small notebooks for each child to document their discoveries. Encourage them to draw pictures of the animals or fossils they see at the museum, or write down interesting facts they learn about desert wildlife and ecosystems.
3. **Desert Treasure Hunt**: Create a simple scavenger hunt list of items like a prickly pear cactus, a butterfly, or a bird's nest. As your family explores the trails, children can check off each item they find, learning about their desert surroundings as they go.

4. **Explorer's Badge Crafting**: After visiting a museum or nature preserve, have a small arts-and-crafts session where kids can create their own explorer badges. Use materials like felt, paper, and markers to design a badge that reflects their favorite part of the adventure.

Tips for Customizing the Itinerary

Every family is unique, and so are their interests. Here are a few tips to make your mini-adventure even more enjoyable and tailored to your needs.

- **For Young Explorers (Ages 3-6)**: Keep the day simple with shorter activities, such as a morning visit to the Natural History Museum, followed by a picnic at Springs Preserve. Bring plenty of water, snacks, and sunscreen to keep little ones comfortable while exploring.
- **For Older Kids (Ages 7-15)**: Older children may enjoy more interactive or challenging experiences. Try extending the trip with a hike at Clark County Wetlands Park or participate in one of the educational workshops often held at Springs Preserve.
- **Combining Discovery and Play**: For families with mixed ages, balance learning with playtime. Plan a visit to nearby parks or playgrounds to give younger children a break while older kids soak up more information at the museum exhibits.
- **Seasonal Considerations**: Las Vegas can be hot in the summer, so opt for early morning or late afternoon outdoor activities. Conversely, cooler winter months make outdoor explorations even more enjoyable. Always check the weather before heading out and dress accordingly.

This chapter of your "Mini-Adventure Planner – Las Vegas, NV-USA Edition" offers a fresh take on Las Vegas, designed to inspire a love of learning and exploration in children while creating unforgettable family memories. Through discovering the hidden wonders of this city, your family will grow closer and leave with not just new knowledge but a deep appreciation for the art of exploration itself.

CHAPTER 2

Adventure 2: Culture & Historic Adventures

Mini-Adventure Planner – Las Vegas, NV-USA Edition

Las Vegas is known for its glitz and glamor, but beneath the bright lights lies a treasure trove of cultural and historical experiences waiting to be explored. In this chapter, we invite families to step into the past, experience vibrant cultural traditions, and learn about the unique history that has shaped this iconic city. Whether your family is spending a few hours or an entire day on this adventure, these activities will immerse you in the heart of Las Vegas' cultural and historical richness.

Itinerary Overview: Exploring Las Vegas' Cultural and Historical Gems

For families looking to delve into the cultural and historical side of Las Vegas, we've crafted flexible half-day and full-day itineraries to suit a variety of schedules. Start your adventure with a visit to **The Neon Museum**, a must-see for any family fascinated by the history of Las Vegas' famous signs. Spend a couple of hours exploring this outdoor museum, where kids can marvel at the vibrant lights that once lit up the Las Vegas Strip. The museum's **Neon Boneyard** is a walk through history, offering a glimpse into the evolution of the city through its iconic signage.

Next, venture to **The Mob Museum**, located in downtown Las Vegas. This interactive museum brings history to life, detailing the fascinating rise of organized crime and its connection to the development of the city. While some exhibits are geared more towards older kids, families can enjoy hands-on activities and storytelling sessions designed for younger audiences. A full-day itinerary might also include a stop at **Springs Preserve**, where families can explore botanical gardens, interactive exhibits on Las Vegas' natural history, and even ride a train that winds through its scenic grounds.

Alternatively, for a more culture-focused day, visit the **Clark County Museum** and the **Hispanic Museum of Nevada**. Both locations highlight the region's deep-rooted heritage and diverse cultural influences. These stops are perfect for younger children, offering interactive exhibits and outdoor spaces for play. Finish your day with a visit to the **Smith Center for the Performing Arts**, where families can attend a family-friendly cultural performance such as a ballet, orchestra, or Broadway-style musical.

Detailed Activities and Experiences

1. **The Neon Museum**
   Location: 770 Las Vegas Blvd N, Las Vegas, NV 89101
   Phone: (702) 387-6366
   Website: www.neonmuseum.org
   Operating Hours: Open daily from 9:00 AM to 10:00 PM.
   The Neon Museum offers a colorful, artistic look at the signs that defined Las Vegas from its early days to the present. The **Neon Boneyard** is perfect for families with young children, who will enjoy spotting the different designs and hearing stories about the city's unique development. Nighttime tours are especially exciting, as several restored signs come to life in the evening glow. Guided tours are available and recommended to get the most out of the experience.

2. **The Mob Museum**
   Location: 300 Stewart Ave, Las Vegas, NV 89101
   Phone: (702) 229-2734
   Website: www.themobmuseum.org
   Operating Hours: Open daily from 9:00 AM to 9:00 PM.
   Known officially as the **National Museum of Organized Crime and Law Enforcement**, The Mob Museum offers fascinating exhibits that tell the story of organized crime in the U.S., with a special focus on Las Vegas. Interactive exhibits include forensic labs, courtroom re-enactments, and a speakeasy experience. While some content is more suited to teens and older children, families with younger kids can explore the museum's storytelling tours that keep history engaging and age-appropriate.

3. **Clark County Museum**
   Location: 1830 S Boulder Hwy, Henderson, NV 89002
   Phone: (702) 455-7955
   Website:
   https://www.clarkcountynv.gov/government/departments/parks__
   _recreation/cultural_division/musuems/clark_county_museum.ph
   p
   Operating Hours: Open daily from 9:00 AM to 4:30 PM.
   The Clark County Museum offers a peek into the area's history, with a large collection of artifacts and restored buildings, such as vintage homes, railcars, and a ghost town setup that kids will love to explore. This museum has a blend of outdoor and indoor exhibits, making it perfect for a variety of weather conditions and interests.

4. **The Hispanic Museum of Nevada**
   Location: 1011 S Main St, Las Vegas, NV 89101
   Phone: (702) 399-8329
   Website: www.hispanicmuseumnv.org
   Operating Hours: Open Tuesday through Saturday from 10:00
   AM to 5:00 PM.
   Focused on the rich Hispanic culture that plays a significant role in
   Las Vegas' history, this museum offers exhibits, workshops, and
   performances that highlight Hispanic heritage and arts. Families can
   participate in traditional craft-making sessions or attend a
   performance showcasing cultural dance or music.

Recommendations for Useful Tools

To enhance your cultural and historical exploration, we recommend
downloading the following apps and tools:

- **Neon Museum App**: This app provides additional information,
  audio tours, and augmented reality features to enhance the museum
  experience.
- **Springs Preserve Interactive Map**: Available on their website, this
  map helps families navigate the various trails, gardens, and exhibits.
- **HistoryPin App**: A great app for kids and families to explore
  historical images and stories of Las Vegas and overlay them with
  modern-day locations.
- **Google Maps**: Essential for families unfamiliar with the layout of
  the city, helping with navigation between the various cultural sites.

Family-friendly Dining Recommendations

No cultural adventure is complete without indulging in some local flavors.
Near your cultural destinations, there are family-friendly dining options
offering a taste of Las Vegas' diverse cuisine:

1. **Luv-It Frozen Custard**
   Location: 505 E Oakey Blvd, Las Vegas, NV 89104
   Hours: Monday-Sunday 1:00 PM – 10:00 PM
   A local favorite, this old-school ice cream stand has been around since 1973, offering creamy frozen custard treats that kids of all ages will love. It's a great stop after a visit to The Neon Museum.

2. **Casa Don Juan**
   Location: 1204 S Main St, Las Vegas, NV 89104
   Hours: Monday-Sunday 8:00 AM – 10:00 PM
   This family-friendly Mexican restaurant is perfect for a meal after exploring the Hispanic Museum. With a wide menu featuring tacos, enchiladas, and kid-friendly dishes, families can enjoy a traditional Mexican dining experience.

3. **The Goodwich**
   Location: 900 S Las Vegas Blvd, Las Vegas, NV 89101
   Hours: Monday-Sunday 8:00 AM – 4:00 PM
   The Goodwich serves up hearty sandwiches and healthy options, perfect for lunch after visiting The Mob Museum or the downtown area. Their menu features both classic and unique sandwich options, ideal for picky eaters.

Creative Memory Makers

To make your family's cultural and historical adventure even more memorable, we suggest engaging in some creative activities. Here are a few unique ideas:

1. **Design Your Own Neon Sign**: After visiting The Neon Museum, kids can create their own paper version of a neon sign using glow-in-the-dark markers or paints. This is a fun way to inspire creativity while reflecting on the history of Vegas' signage.

2. **Journal the Past**: Encourage kids to write a journal entry or draw a picture of their favorite cultural experience from the day. Provide prompts like "What did you learn about the history of Las Vegas today?" or "If you could live in any of the houses from the Clark County Museum, which one would it be and why?"

3. **Attend a Cultural Performance**: The **Smith Center** often hosts kid-friendly performances that introduce families to different musical and cultural traditions. After attending a show, encourage kids to share their favorite part and what they learned about the culture represented in the performance.

Tips for Customizing the Itinerary

Families with younger children may prefer to focus on activities with interactive or outdoor elements. For example, if your children are preschool age, consider spending more time at Springs Preserve, which offers plenty of space to run around and explore nature in a hands-on way. Older children may enjoy the historical storytelling at The Mob Museum or getting involved in a craft workshop at the Hispanic Museum.

When planning your trip, consider visiting one cultural site in the morning and enjoying a leisurely lunch before continuing your journey. Most of the destinations listed in this chapter are located relatively close to one another, making it easy to structure your day without extensive travel.

If your family enjoys nighttime adventures, try the evening tour at The Neon Museum. It's a magical way to end the day, especially when the neon lights come alive after dark.

Chapter 3

Adventure 3: Outdoor Adventures

Mini-Adventure Planner – Las Vegas, NV-USA Edition

Las Vegas may be synonymous with neon lights and casinos, but families can also experience a wealth of natural beauty and outdoor adventures just beyond the Strip. In this chapter, we focus on exhilarating outdoor activities that provide families with fun and adventure in nature. From rugged desert landscapes to scenic parks and adrenaline-pumping activities, this guide highlights the best places to explore the great outdoors in and around Las Vegas, perfect for children ages 3 to 15.

Itinerary Overview: Exploring the Outdoors Around Las Vegas

Las Vegas offers a variety of outdoor activities that can be enjoyed over half-day or full-day adventures, depending on your family's pace and preferences. For a morning or afternoon trip, start with a visit to **Red Rock Canyon National Conservation Area**, a must-see for families who love hiking and scenic views. The various trails offer something for every skill level, from easy, child-friendly paths to more challenging hikes for adventurous families.

If your family is interested in discovering unique flora and fauna, the **Spring Mountain Ranch State Park** provides a perfect opportunity. Spend a half-day exploring the grassy meadows, streams, and historical ranch buildings before enjoying a picnic under the desert sky. For a full-day outdoor adventure, combine Red Rock Canyon with a trip to **Floyd Lamb Park**, where you can stroll around tranquil lakes, visit historic ranch houses, and even spot wildlife like peacocks and rabbits.

For adrenaline-loving families, add some excitement to your itinerary by visiting **Bootleg Canyon**, where you can ride one of the thrilling zipline courses that send you soaring over the desert landscape. Alternatively, plan a full-day outing to **Lake Mead National Recreation Area**, where families can enjoy water activities like kayaking, paddleboarding, and swimming while surrounded by stunning views of the desert mountains.

Detailed Activities and Experiences

1. **Red Rock Canyon National Conservation Area**
   Location: 1000 Scenic Loop Dr, Las Vegas, NV 89161
   Phone: (702) 515-5350
   Website: www.redrockcanyonlv.org
   Operating Hours: Open daily from 6:00 AM to 7:00 PM
   This outdoor gem is just a short drive from Las Vegas, offering families a chance to explore the beauty of the Mojave Desert. With numerous hiking trails ranging from easy walks for younger kids to more strenuous paths for older children and teens, Red Rock Canyon is a great spot for active families. Be sure to stop by the visitor center, where kids can learn about the local wildlife and geological features of the area.

2. **Spring Mountain Ranch State Park**
   Location: 6375 NV-159, Blue Diamond, NV 89004
   Phone: (702) 875-4141
   Website: https://parks.nv.gov/events
   Operating Hours: Open daily from 8:00 AM to 5:00 PM
   This historic state park offers a peaceful retreat from the city. Families can hike, picnic, and even explore the historic ranch house that dates back to the early 1800s. The park also hosts occasional living history demonstrations, where kids can learn about Nevada's pioneer past in a fun and interactive way.

3. **Floyd Lamb Park**
   Location: 9200 Tule Springs Rd, Las Vegas, NV 89131
   Phone: (702) 229-8100
   Website: www.lasvegasnevada.gov
   Operating Hours: Open daily from 7:00 AM to 7:00 PM
   Floyd Lamb Park is a family favorite, with its serene lakes, picnic
   areas, and walking trails. It's an ideal spot for younger children to
   run around and explore nature. Families can also visit the historic
   Tule Springs Ranch, which offers a glimpse into Nevada's past, or
   simply relax by the water while spotting local wildlife.

4. **Bootleg Canyon Zipline Tours**
   Location: 1644 Boulder City Pkwy, Boulder City, NV 89005
   Phone: (702) 293-6885
   Website: www.flightlinezbootleg.com
   Operating Hours: Tours available daily from 8:00 AM to 5:00 PM
   For families seeking a thrill, Bootleg Canyon offers zipline tours that
   provide breathtaking views of the desert landscape as you zip from
   one peak to another. This activity is best suited for older kids and
   teens, but it's an exhilarating way to explore the great outdoors and
   add a sense of adventure to your day.

5. **Lake Mead National Recreation Area**
   Location: 10 Lakeshore Rd, Boulder City, NV 89005
   Phone: (702) 293-8990
   Website: https://www.nps.gov/lake/planyourvisit/basicinfo.htm
   Operating Hours: Open 24 hours daily
   Lake Mead offers a wide range of outdoor activities, from swimming and boating to hiking and picnicking. Families can rent kayaks or paddle boards for an on-the-water adventure, or stick to the shore for some wildlife spotting and nature photography. With plenty of picnic areas and shaded spots, it's an ideal destination for a full day of outdoor fun.

Recommendations for Useful Tools

To make your family's outdoor adventure even more enjoyable, here are some useful tools and apps:

- **AllTrails**: This app provides trail maps, difficulty levels, and user reviews for hiking trails, including those at Red Rock Canyon and Spring Mountain Ranch.
- **National Park Service App**: The NPS app provides information about Lake Mead and other parks, including maps, ranger programs, and wildlife spotting guides.
- **REI Co-op Rentals**: If your family needs outdoor gear, REI offers rental services for equipment like kayaks, tents, and mountain bikes, making it easy to gear up for your adventure.

Family-friendly Dining Recommendations

After a day of outdoor fun, refuel at one of these family-friendly dining spots that offer great views and relaxing atmospheres:

1. **Cottonwood Station Eatery**
   Location: 8972 NV-160, Blue Diamond, NV 89004
   Hours: Tuesday-Sunday, 7:30 AM to 4:00 PM
   This charming café is located near Red Rock Canyon and Spring Mountain Ranch, making it a great place to stop for breakfast or lunch. They offer fresh sandwiches, pizzas, and baked goods, perfect for a post-hike meal.

2. **The Water Street Pizzeria**
   Location: 223 S Water St, Henderson, NV 89015
   Hours: Monday-Sunday, 11:00 AM to 9:00 PM
   This family-friendly pizzeria in Henderson is a great place to unwind after an adventure-filled day. Their menu features a variety of pizzas and pastas, with plenty of kid-friendly options.

3. **The Big Horn Café**
   Location: 711 Casino Dr, Boulder City, NV 89005 (inside Hoover Dam Lodge)
   Hours: Open 24 hours
   Located near Lake Mead, this café offers casual dining with a wide variety of dishes to suit all tastes. It's a perfect stop after a day at the lake, offering burgers, salads, and comfort food in a relaxed setting.

Creative Memory Makers

Make your family's outdoor adventure even more memorable with these fun activities:

1. **Nature Scavenger Hunt**: Create a scavenger hunt for your kids as you explore places like Red Rock Canyon or Floyd Lamb Park. Ask them to find specific plants, rocks, or animals, helping them connect with nature while learning about the local ecosystem.

2. **Outdoor Family Games**: At Spring Mountain Ranch or Lake Mead, organize some fun family games such as frisbee, sack races, or even water balloon tosses. These activities are perfect for burning off energy and building family bonds.

3. **Rock Art and Souvenirs**: Encourage your kids to collect small, smooth stones during your hikes. Once you're home, they can decorate them with paints or markers to create their own personalized "rock art" as a memento of the adventure.

Safety Tips

Safety is paramount when exploring the outdoors, especially in the desert environment around Las Vegas. Keep these tips in mind:

- **Stay Hydrated**: Always bring plenty of water, especially during the hotter months. Desert heat can be extreme, so ensure everyone in the family drinks regularly.
- **Wear Sunscreen and Hats**: The sun in Las Vegas can be intense, so protect your family's skin by applying sunscreen and wearing wide-brimmed hats.
- **Watch for Wildlife**: While exploring areas like Red Rock Canyon, be mindful of desert wildlife, including snakes and lizards. Teach your children to observe animals from a safe distance.
- **Check the Weather**: Before heading out, check the weather forecast and avoid outdoor activities if extreme heat or storms are expected.

Tips for Customizing the Itinerary

Families with younger children may prefer to focus on activities that involve less strenuous physical exertion, such as walking the shorter, flatter trails at Red Rock Canyon or enjoying a picnic at Floyd Lamb Park. For families with older children, combining hiking with a high-adrenaline activity like the Bootleg Canyon zipline can make for an exciting day.

When planning your adventure, consider the weather and time of day. Mornings and evenings are the best times to explore the desert areas, as temperatures are cooler. For water-based activities, mid-day might be more appropriate to enjoy the sun while cooling off in Lake Mead's waters.

By taking the time to plan and customize your family's outdoor adventure, you can ensure an enjoyable, active, and safe experience for everyone.

Chapter 4

Adventure 4: Creativity & The Arts

Mini-Adventure Planner – Las Vegas, NV-USA Edition

Las Vegas is a city bursting with artistic energy and creative expression. Beyond the glittering lights and entertainment spectacles, families can immerse themselves in unique artistic experiences that showcase the city's thriving arts scene. In this chapter, we'll take you through the must-see art galleries, performances, hands-on workshops, and cultural venues perfect for children ages 3 to 15. From exploring colorful murals to participating in craft workshops, this artistic adventure will spark creativity in children and inspire families to connect through the power of art.

Itinerary Overview: Creative Escapes in Las Vegas

For families interested in creativity and the arts, this chapter provides both half-day and full-day itineraries filled with opportunities to engage in hands-on activities and enjoy the artistic vibe of Las Vegas. Start your day with a visit to the **Las Vegas Arts District**, a vibrant neighborhood filled with street art, galleries, and unique creative spaces. Here, you'll find the perfect blend of interactive exhibits for kids and visually stunning works that will captivate the whole family.

Next, make your way to the **Smith Center for the Performing Arts** for a family-friendly theater production, concert, or dance performance. With shows and programs designed for young audiences, this venue offers a wonderful opportunity for children to experience the performing arts in a lively, welcoming environment.

For a full-day itinerary, combine the Arts District and a stop at **DISCOVERY Children's Museum**, where creativity and imagination take center stage. This interactive museum offers plenty of hands-on exhibits and creative spaces for kids to build, design, and explore, fostering their artistic abilities in a fun and educational environment.

Detailed Activities and Experiences

1. **Las Vegas Arts District**
   Location: Main St & Charleston Blvd, Las Vegas, NV 89104
   Website: www.18bartsdistrict.com
   The Las Vegas Arts District is the cultural heart of the city, home to a thriving artistic community. Families can stroll through streets lined with colorful murals, visit small galleries showcasing local and international art, and even participate in occasional workshops. The first Friday of each month brings **First Friday Las Vegas**, a vibrant art walk with live performances, food trucks, and family-friendly art activities.

2. **The Smith Center for the Performing Arts**
   Location: 361 Symphony Park Ave, Las Vegas, NV 89106
   Phone: (702) 749-2000
   Website: www.thesmithcenter.com
   Operating Hours: Performances vary, check website for schedule.
   The Smith Center hosts an array of performances suitable for families, from kid-friendly musicals to orchestral concerts and ballet performances. With youth-focused programming like **Disney in Concert** or **Peter and the Wolf**, the center ensures that even the youngest audience members can enjoy the magic of live performance. Be sure to check the calendar for family specials and matinee shows.

3. **DISCOVERY Children's Museum**
   Location: 360 Promenade Place, Las Vegas, NV 89106
   Phone: (702) 382-3445
   Website: www.discoverykidslv.org
   Operating Hours: Tuesday-Saturday, 10:00 AM to 5:00 PM
   This interactive museum is a must for families with young children who want to engage in creative learning. With exhibits like **Fantasy Festival**, where kids can dress up and perform in a castle-themed setting, or **Eco City**, where they can design and build eco-friendly communities, the museum offers plenty of opportunities for creative exploration.

4. **Bellagio Gallery of Fine Art**
   Location: 3600 S Las Vegas Blvd, Las Vegas, NV 89109 (Inside the Bellagio Hotel)
   Phone: (702) 693-7871
   Website: www.bellagio.com
   Operating Hours: Daily from 10:00 AM to 6:00 PM
   For families interested in fine art, the Bellagio Gallery of Fine Art is a hidden gem on the Strip. Exhibits rotate frequently, showcasing works from world-renowned artists such as Picasso, Warhol, and more. While more suited to older children, the gallery often features family-friendly guides and educational programs that make art more accessible to younger visitors.

5. **Color Me Mine Las Vegas**
   Location: 9350 W Sahara Ave #110, Las Vegas, NV 89117
   Phone: (702) 522-7119
   Website: www.colormemine.com
   Operating Hours: Daily from 11:00 AM to 7:00 PM
   This hands-on pottery painting studio is perfect for families who
   want to create something artistic together. Choose a piece of
   pottery—whether it's a mug, plate, or figurine—and let your
   creativity flow as you paint your design. The studio staff will glaze
   and fire your creation, allowing you to take home a unique piece of
   art that your family created together.

Recommendations for Useful Tools

Enhance your artistic adventure in Las Vegas with these helpful tools and apps:

- **First Friday Las Vegas App**: Stay updated on upcoming art walks, performances, and interactive events in the Las Vegas Arts District. This app provides schedules and highlights of the best family-friendly activities happening during the popular First Friday events.
- **Las Vegas Arts District Guide**: Available on the district's website, this guide helps families navigate galleries, art installations, and street art locations. The guide also lists special workshops and exhibits happening in the area.
- **Bellagio Gallery of Fine Art Audio Tour**: Download the audio tour for the Bellagio Gallery of Fine Art to hear in-depth explanations about the artwork on display, making it easier for kids and adults to connect with the exhibits.

Family-friendly Dining Recommendations

After a day filled with creative exploration, treat your family to a meal at one of these artistic dining spots:

1. **True Food Kitchen**
   Location: 10970 Rosemary Park Dr, Las Vegas, NV 89135
   Hours: Monday-Sunday, 11:00 AM to 9:00 PM
   This health-conscious restaurant in Summerlin is perfect for families looking for a nutritious meal after a day of artistic adventures. The open, modern dining area is filled with natural light, creating a refreshing and creative ambiance. They offer a variety of kid-friendly options made from fresh, organic ingredients.

2. **Sugar Factory**
   Location: 3200 S Las Vegas Blvd, Las Vegas, NV 89109
   Hours: Monday-Sunday, 11:00 AM to 11:00 PM
   A whimsical spot for families with a sweet tooth, Sugar Factory is known for its over-the-top desserts and candy-themed décor. Kids will love the artistic presentation of the treats, from massive milkshakes to colorful candy displays, making it a perfect end to a fun-filled creative day.

Creative Memory Makers

Capture and enhance your family's artistic adventure in Las Vegas with these creative activities:

1. **Family Art Journals**: Encourage your kids to keep a creative journal during your visit. They can draw sketches of their favorite murals, create collages with gallery brochures, or write about their experience at the pottery studio. This is a great way to reflect on the trip while fostering creative expression.

2. **Collaborative Family Art Project**: After visiting Color Me Mine, take inspiration from your pottery creation and work together on a family art project at home. Use different mediums like painting, crafting, or even photography to create a collaborative piece of art that symbolizes your trip.

3. **Mini Performance Show**: After attending a performance at The Smith Center, encourage your kids to put on their own mini-show at home. They can use costumes, create their own scripts, and reenact their favorite scenes from the performance. It's a fun way to inspire creativity while building confidence and storytelling skills.

Tips for Customizing the Itinerary

For younger children, focus on hands-on activities like visiting the DISCOVERY Children's Museum and participating in a workshop at Color Me Mine. These experiences offer plenty of opportunities for creative play and expression in a relaxed setting. For families with older children, combine an arts district walk with a stop at the Bellagio Gallery of Fine Art or a more mature theater performance at The Smith Center.

To make the most of your day, plan your visit around the **First Friday** art walk if you're in town on the first weekend of the month. This event offers live music, food, and plenty of family-friendly activities in the Arts District, providing a great atmosphere for both younger and older kids to enjoy.

By customizing your itinerary based on your family's interests and energy levels, you can create a day filled with creativity, inspiration, and lifelong memories.

Las Vegas is a city of endless creativity, and this chapter is designed to inspire families to explore and engage with its artistic side. Whether you're crafting, watching performances, or simply strolling through the city's art districts, there are plenty of opportunities to spark the imaginations of children and adults alike.

Chapter 5

Adventure 5: The Foodie Family

Mini-Adventure Planner – Las Vegas, NV-USA Edition

Las Vegas, renowned for its extravagant shows and larger-than-life attractions, is also a paradise for food lovers. Families visiting Las Vegas can experience the city's diverse culinary scene, which offers something for every palate. Whether your family enjoys savoring international cuisines, sampling local food markets, or getting hands-on with cooking classes, this chapter offers a comprehensive guide to culinary delights. With half-day and full-day itinerary options, families can explore local food tours, dine in family-friendly restaurants, and make lasting memories through food-focused experiences.

Itinerary Overview: A Day of Culinary Exploration

For a half-day culinary adventure, start your morning with a visit to the **Las Vegas Farmers Market** in Summerlin. This vibrant market offers a wide range of fresh, locally grown produce and artisanal foods that your family can sample or take back to your accommodation. Follow this up with lunch at **Pizza Rock**, a lively pizzeria downtown, where kids can indulge in gourmet pizzas while enjoying the restaurant's fun atmosphere.

For a full-day foodie experience, combine your morning at the farmers market with an afternoon food tour. The **Lip Smacking Foodie Tour** offers family-friendly options that allow you to explore a range of restaurants and taste signature dishes from various chefs. After the tour, consider attending a family cooking class at the **Las Vegas School of Cooking**, where you and your kids can work together to prepare a meal with the guidance of a professional chef.

Detailed Activities and Experiences

1. **Las Vegas Farmers Market**
   Location: 7650 W Sahara Ave, Las Vegas, NV 89117
   Phone: (702) 832-1000
   Website: www.lasvegasfarmersmarket.com
   Operating Hours: Wednesdays, 2:00 PM to 8:00 PM
   Las Vegas Farmers Market provides an authentic experience for families looking to sample locally grown produce and handmade foods. Kids can explore different stalls offering fresh fruits, honey, and baked goods, while parents can shop for gourmet ingredients and homemade jams. The market also hosts live music and food trucks, creating a festive atmosphere that the whole family will enjoy.

2. **Pizza Rock**
   Location: 201 N 3rd St, Las Vegas, NV 89101
   Phone: (702) 385-0838
   Website: www.pizzarocklasvegas.com
   Operating Hours: Daily from 11:00 AM to 10:00 PM
   A must-visit for pizza lovers, Pizza Rock is famous for its wood-fired
   pizzas and innovative toppings. The restaurant's lively atmosphere,
   complete with rock music and neon signs, makes it an entertaining
   dining option for families. Kids can build their own pizzas or enjoy
   classic options like Margherita, while parents can sample more
   adventurous selections.

3. **Lip Smacking Foodie Tour**
   Location: Multiple locations along the Las Vegas Strip
   Phone: (888) 681-4388
   Website: www.lipsmackingfoodietours.com
   Operating Hours: Times vary; reservations required
   The Lip Smacking Foodie Tour offers curated culinary experiences
   for families looking to explore the best of Las Vegas's dining scene.
   The tour includes stops at several top-rated restaurants where
   families can sample everything from gourmet appetizers to signature
   desserts. Each tour is guided by knowledgeable hosts who share
   stories about the chefs and the history behind the dishes, making it
   an educational as well as a delicious experience.

4. **Las Vegas School of Cooking**
   Location: 6115 S Fort Apache Rd, Suite 104, Las Vegas, NV 89148
   Phone: (702) 688-0644
   Website: www.lvcooking.com
   Operating Hours: Classes by appointment; check website for availability. This hands-on cooking school is a great way for families to bond over a shared love of food. With classes designed for all ages and skill levels, kids can learn to make their favorite dishes from scratch, whether it's pizza, pasta, or desserts. The classes are interactive, encouraging kids to participate in every step of the process, from chopping ingredients to plating the finished dish.

5. **Viva Las Arepas**
   Location: 1616 S Las Vegas Blvd, Las Vegas, NV 89104
   Phone: (702) 366-9696
   Website: www.vivalasarepas.com
   Operating Hours: Monday-Sunday, 10:00 AM to 8:00 PM
   For families looking to explore international cuisine, Viva Las
   Arepas offers authentic Venezuelan street food in a casual,
   family-friendly setting. Their signature dish, the arepa, is a cornmeal
   patty stuffed with savory fillings like shredded beef or grilled
   chicken. The restaurant's relaxed atmosphere and affordable menu
   make it an ideal stop for families exploring the Strip.

Recommendations for Useful Tools

To enhance your family's foodie adventure in Las Vegas, consider using
these helpful tools:

- **Yelp**: With Yelp, you can find reviews and recommendations for
  family-friendly restaurants in Las Vegas. The app allows you to
  search by cuisine, location, and user ratings, helping you choose the
  best spots to dine with kids.
- **OpenTable**: This app is perfect for making reservations at popular
  Las Vegas restaurants, ensuring you get a table without a long wait.
  You can filter by family-friendly options and special menus for kids.
- **HappyCow**: For families with vegetarian or vegan dietary
  preferences, HappyCow is an excellent app to find restaurants that
  cater to plant-based diets. It provides detailed information about
  vegan options at various Las Vegas eateries.
- **AllergyEats**: For families dealing with food allergies, this app helps
  you identify restaurants that are allergy-friendly, ensuring a safe and
  enjoyable dining experience.

Tips for Families with Dietary Restrictions

Las Vegas has a diverse food scene, and many restaurants cater to dietary restrictions, making it easy for families with food allergies, gluten-free, or vegan diets to enjoy their meals. Here are some tips for managing dietary needs while exploring the city:

- **Gluten-Free Options**: Many restaurants in Las Vegas offer gluten-free menus or can accommodate gluten-free requests. For pizza lovers, Pizza Rock has a gluten-free pizza option, while restaurants like **Honey Salt** and **Lago by Julian Serrano** offer gluten-free dishes for both kids and adults.
- **Vegan and Vegetarian**: Las Vegas is home to several vegan and vegetarian restaurants, such as **VegeNation**, which serves plant-based global dishes, and **Tacotarian**, which specializes in vegan tacos. For families exploring the Strip, these restaurants provide tasty alternatives to traditional dining options.
- **Picky Eaters**: For families with picky eaters, dining at restaurants with customizable menus is key. Places like **Eataly Las Vegas** allow kids to build their own pasta dishes or pizzas, while many burger joints offer build-your-own burgers to satisfy even the most selective eaters.

Family-friendly Dining Recommendations

Las Vegas offers a variety of family-friendly dining spots where kids and parents can enjoy delicious meals together. Here are some must-visit restaurants integrated with your culinary activities:

1. **Black Tap Craft Burgers & Beer**
   Location: 3355 S Las Vegas Blvd, Las Vegas, NV 89109 (Inside The Venetian)
   Phone: (702) 414-2337
   Website: www.blacktap.com
   Black Tap is famous for its over-the-top milkshakes and gourmet burgers. The kid-friendly atmosphere and fun menu make it a great choice for families. Parents can enjoy craft beers while kids indulge in sweet treats like the **Cotton Candy Shake** or **CrazyShake**.

2. **The Crack Shack**
   Location: 3778 S Las Vegas Blvd, Las Vegas, NV 89109 (The Park MGM)
   Phone: (702) 820-5991
   Website: www.crackshack.com
   This family-friendly spot specializes in fried chicken and creative chicken sandwiches. With a playful atmosphere and outdoor seating, The Crack Shack is perfect for a relaxed family meal after a busy day exploring the Strip.

Creative Memory Makers

Make the most of your family's foodie adventure by incorporating some creative memory-making activities into your day:

1. **Family Recipe Book**: Encourage your kids to collect recipes from the dishes they enjoyed most during the trip. After trying new foods at restaurants or cooking together in classes, write down the recipes and compile them into a family recipe book. Include notes about your favorite meals and photos of your culinary creations.

2. **Food Photography Challenge**: Turn your family's culinary adventure into a fun photography challenge. Encourage each family member to take pictures of the food they order, and then vote on the best photo at the end of the day. Categories could include "Most Colorful Dish" or "Best Dessert Shot."

3. **Cooking at Home**: After participating in a cooking class or visiting a farmers market, take what you've learned home. Challenge your family to recreate one of the dishes from the trip, and host a family cooking night where everyone plays a role in preparing the meal.

Tips for Customizing the Itinerary

To make the most out of your culinary adventure, consider these tips for customizing your itinerary based on your family's preferences and time constraints:

- **For Younger Kids**: Focus on hands-on experiences like cooking classes or visiting casual, interactive dining spots where children can participate, such as Pizza Rock or Eataly. These experiences allow younger kids to get involved in the food-making process, which can keep them engaged throughout the day.

- **For Older Kids and Teens**: Consider adding more food tours or food-related workshops that explore the history of different cuisines in Las Vegas. Older children may enjoy learning about the origins of some of the city's iconic dishes while sampling different foods along the way.

- **For Families with Limited Time**: If you're short on time, prioritize a half-day visit to the Las Vegas Farmers Market, followed by lunch at a family-friendly restaurant like Viva Las Arepas. This condensed itinerary still provides a taste of Las Vegas's diverse food culture without taking up an entire day.

By customizing your foodie adventure based on your family's interests and preferences, you can ensure that everyone has an enjoyable and memorable experience filled with delicious food and exciting activities.

Las Vegas's culinary scene is full of surprises, and by taking the time to explore it with your family, you'll create memories that last long after the trip is over. Whether it's trying new foods, learning to cook, or simply enjoying a great meal together, this chapter will guide you through the best family-friendly food experiences the city has to offer.

Chapter 6

Adventure 6: Science & Education Trail

For families seeking a blend of learning and fun, Las Vegas offers a wealth of educational adventures that go beyond the well-known attractions. The **Science & Education Trail** invites children and parents alike to explore lesser-known gems that spark curiosity, encourage problem-solving, and expand horizons. This trail is perfect for families with children aged 3-15 and can accommodate both half-day and full-day adventures, depending on how much learning and discovery you'd like to pack into your day.

Itinerary Overview: Discovering Las Vegas' Educational Side

For a **half-day itinerary**, begin with a morning trip to **Lied Discovery Children's Academy**—not to be confused with the Discovery Children's Museum, this academy offers workshops and interactive science exhibits designed to teach younger kids about STEM in a hands-on environment. Afterward, head to the **University of Nevada, Las Vegas (UNLV) Planetarium**, where families can explore astronomy through interactive shows and viewings of the night sky.

For a **full-day itinerary**, add a visit to **Techatticup Mine** in Nelson, a short drive from Las Vegas. This historical site offers guided tours of Nevada's oldest gold mine, along with lessons in geology and mining technology. The educational aspect is coupled with a bit of outdoor exploration, giving families a chance to learn and hike at the same time. Wrap up the day at **Las Vegas Mini Grand Prix**, where STEM meets speed, teaching children the science behind karting.

Detailed Activities and Experiences

1. Lied Discovery Children's Academy

Location: 7250 Peak Dr, Las Vegas, NV 89128
Phone: (702) 255-5437
Website: www.ldcakids.org
Operating Hours: Monday to Saturday, 9:00 AM to 5:00 PM

Lied Discovery Children's Academy is a hidden treasure for younger children who have a passion for science and creativity. The academy is filled with STEM-focused exhibits that invite children to explore physics, biology, and robotics in a highly interactive environment. Special workshops on coding, space exploration, and nature studies are available, offering a chance for hands-on learning. The academy frequently hosts "Young Inventors" sessions where children can design their own creations using simple engineering principles.

2. UNLV Planetarium

Location: 4505 S Maryland Pkwy, Las Vegas, NV 89154
Phone: (702) 895-3394
Website: www.unlv.edu/planetarium
Operating Hours: Tuesday to Friday, 10:00 AM to 4:00 PM

UNLV Planetarium brings the mysteries of the universe closer to home with its state-of-the-art dome theater and celestial displays. The planetarium offers several educational programs for families, including "Astronomy for Beginners," which walks children through the basics of star-gazing and solar system exploration. There are also special events such as lunar observation nights and meteor shower viewing parties. After a visit, kids will walk away with a greater appreciation for the stars above them and an understanding of how astronomers study space.

3. Techatticup Mine and Eldorado Canyon

Location: 16880 NV-165, Nelson, NV 89046
Phone: (702) 291-0026
Website: www.eldoradocanyonminetours.com
Operating Hours: Daily, 8:00 AM to 6:00 PM

For a taste of history combined with geology, visit **Techatticup Mine**, located about 45 minutes outside of Las Vegas. This guided tour offers an in-depth look at the gold mining operations of the late 1800s and teaches visitors about the tools and techniques used by miners of the time. Children will enjoy learning about geology, as the guides explain how various types of rocks and minerals were discovered in the area. There's also a great outdoor element—families can explore the beautiful surroundings of Eldorado Canyon and learn about desert ecosystems while they're at it.

4. Las Vegas Mini Grand Prix

Location: 1401 N Rainbow Blvd, Las Vegas, NV 89108
Phone: (702) 259-7000
Website: www.lvmgp.com
Operating Hours: Daily, 10:00 AM to 9:00 PM

For a science-meets-sports experience, **Las Vegas Mini Grand Prix** offers children the chance to learn about physics while enjoying the thrill of karting. This family-friendly venue has STEM-themed educational programs that explain the science of speed, friction, and aerodynamics in a way that's fun and accessible for kids. After a brief lesson, they can hop into a mini go-kart to put their newly learned knowledge into practice on the racetrack. It's a great way to combine learning with some active, physical fun.

5. The Escape Game Las Vegas

Location: 3500 Las Vegas Blvd S, Las Vegas, NV 89109
Phone: (702) 710-8144
Website: www.theescapegame.com/lasvegas
Operating Hours: Daily, 10:00 AM to 11:00 PM

For a hands-on science challenge, visit **The Escape Game Las Vegas**, where families can work together to solve puzzles and unlock clues in a series of themed escape rooms. These interactive games test critical thinking, teamwork, and problem-solving skills, making them a fun and educational activity for older kids and teens. Themes include space missions, art heists, and even time travel, blending storytelling with STEM-based puzzles that engage the whole family in a mental challenge.

Recommendations for Useful Tools

- **SkyView Lite**: This free app allows families to point their phones toward the sky and identify constellations, planets, and other celestial objects—perfect for an evening under the stars after visiting the UNLV Planetarium.
- **Geocaching App**: For use at the Clark County Wetlands Park, this app turns your outdoor adventure into a treasure hunt where children can use GPS to locate hidden geocaches in the park.
- **Physics Karting App**: This educational app, available at Las Vegas Mini Grand Prix, helps children understand the principles of motion and speed through karting simulations before they get behind the wheel.

Family-Friendly Dining Recommendations

Las Vegas is full of diverse, family-friendly restaurants that cater to all ages and dietary preferences. Here are some fresh recommendations for dining locations where kids and parents alike can enjoy a memorable meal after a day of exploring.

1. **Buddy V's Ristorante**
   Location: 3327 S Las Vegas Blvd, Las Vegas, NV 89109
   Phone: (702) 607-2355
   Website: www.buddyvsrestaurants.com
   Located in the Grand Canal Shoppes at The Venetian, this restaurant by the "Cake Boss" Buddy Valastro offers classic Italian comfort food that kids and adults will love. The menu is packed with delicious pizzas, pastas, and kid-sized meals, while the dessert menu includes treats that will wow children, such as massive cannolis and decadent tiramisu. The casual, family-friendly atmosphere makes it a great spot for dinner after a day of discovery.

2. **The Yard House**
   Location: 3545 Las Vegas Blvd S, Las Vegas, NV 89109
   Phone: (702) 597-0434
   Website: www.yardhouse.com
   Famous for its wide-ranging American menu, Yard House is a great spot for families looking for variety. They offer everything from burgers to salads to pasta dishes, and a special kids' menu ensures there's something for everyone. The large portions and fun ambiance make it a perfect choice for big families or those with hearty appetites.

3. **Lazy Dog Restaurant & Bar**
   Location: 6509 S Las Vegas Blvd, Las Vegas, NV 89119
   Phone: (702) 941-1920
   Website: www.lazydogrestaurants.com
   Lazy Dog is a relaxed spot that feels more like a cozy, neighborhood hangout than a restaurant on the Strip. They offer a kids' menu featuring smaller portions of their hearty American meals, and their outdoor seating is pet-friendly, perfect for families traveling with furry friends. Dishes like pot roast, stir fry, and wood-fired pizzas will satisfy every member of the family.

4. **Black Bear Diner**
   Location: 6180 W Tropicana Ave, Las Vegas, NV 89103
   Phone: (702) 368-1077
   Website: www.blackbeardiner.com
   Known for its large portions and down-home comfort food, Black Bear Diner offers breakfast all day, along with classic diner fare like burgers, sandwiches, and meatloaf. The kid's menu is extensive, with options like "cub" pancakes, grilled cheese, and spaghetti. Its friendly service and welcoming atmosphere make it a family favorite for those looking for a casual, hearty meal.

Creative Memory Makers

- **Create Your Own Fossil**: After visiting Techatticup Mine, take a piece of the experience home by creating DIY fossils with clay and leaves or shells. This is a great way for younger children to learn about geology while crafting.
- **Start a Birdwatching Journal**: At Clark County Wetlands Park, families can start a birdwatching journal, jotting down different species they spot during their visit. This encourages kids to connect with nature and learn about the diversity of bird species in the area.
- **Build a Go-Kart Model**: Following a fun day at the Las Vegas Mini Grand Prix, families can bond over building a simple go-kart model kit at home, continuing the lesson on engineering and motion.

Tips for Customizing the Itinerary

- **For Younger Kids**: Focus on hands-on experiences like the Lied Discovery Children's Academy and a relaxed visit to the Clark County Wetlands Park for guided nature walks.
- **For Older Kids**: Incorporate more advanced educational experiences like the UNLV Planetarium or a full exploration of Techatticup Mine, which delves into geology and history.
- **For Families with Limited Time**: Choose shorter, more focused experiences like a trip to the UNLV Planetarium and Las Vegas Mini Grand Prix for a day filled with both learning and active fun.

This **Science & Education Trail** is an immersive adventure filled with unique learning experiences that go beyond the textbook. Each destination provides a hands-on approach to science, nature, and history, ensuring that children and families leave with a deeper understanding of the world around them.

Chapter 7

Planning Your Adventure

Preparing for Your Trip

When planning a family adventure to Las Vegas, preparation is key to ensuring a smooth and fun-filled trip. Whether it's packing the essentials, making sure your itinerary is family-friendly, or knowing what to expect once you arrive, thoughtful planning can turn a good vacation into a great one. Here's a detailed guide to help you plan your Las Vegas adventure, with tips and tricks specifically designed for families with children aged 3-15.

Pack Smart for All Occasions

Las Vegas is known for its diverse climate and activities, so packing for various scenarios is important. The desert climate means the city experiences hot summers and cooler winters. Here's a checklist of must-haves for a family trip:

- **Water Bottles**: Staying hydrated is crucial, especially during the hot summer months.
- **Sunscreen & Hats**: The sun can be intense, so packing SPF and sun protection is essential.
- **Layered Clothing**: Bring light, breathable clothing for daytime adventures, but remember that evenings can get chilly, especially if you're venturing into the surrounding desert areas or higher altitudes like Red Rock Canyon.
- **Comfy Shoes**: You'll be walking a lot, whether it's on the Strip, exploring museums, or hiking. Comfortable shoes are a must for both kids and adults.
- **Entertainment for the Kids**: Las Vegas can be overstimulating, so it's helpful to have some quieter activities—like books, coloring supplies, or handheld games—on hand for down moments.

Involve Your Kids in the Planning Process

One of the best ways to get kids excited about the trip is to involve them in the planning. Ask your children what they're most excited about. Whether it's visiting a particular museum, going on a hike, or trying out new foods, letting them have a say can build anticipation.

For younger kids, you can make a fun, visual checklist of the activities planned for each day. Use pictures of the places you'll be visiting and let them cross off each activity as the day goes on. This can also help keep the trip organized while giving children a sense of accomplishment.

Budgeting for Your Trip

Las Vegas offers activities that fit all kinds of budgets, but it's always helpful to have an idea of what you're willing to spend before your trip. Here's a simple guide to help:

- **Accommodation**: From budget-friendly hotels to all-inclusive family resorts, Las Vegas has a wide range of accommodation options. Some resorts offer kid-friendly pools and game rooms, making them perfect for a family stay.
- **Activities**: Many of the best family activities are affordable or free, such as exploring the parks and public art in the Downtown Arts District. However, attractions like museums, tours, and shows may require ticket purchases, so it's important to set aside some funds for these experiences.
- **Food**: With a variety of dining options—from quick bites to sit-down family-friendly restaurants—plan a budget that allows you to enjoy the diverse culinary experiences Las Vegas offers without breaking the bank.

Navigating the City

Las Vegas is a bustling city, and getting from one point to another can sometimes be a bit overwhelming, especially when you're traveling with children. But fear not! The city offers numerous convenient transportation options to help you and your family navigate its streets with ease.

Public Transportation

Las Vegas has a well-connected public transportation system that makes it easy to explore the city, especially if you're staying on or near the Strip.

- **The Deuce**: This double-decker bus is one of the most popular ways to get around the Strip. It operates 24/7 and stops at most major hotels and attractions. It's a great option if you're looking to explore without worrying about parking.
- **Monorail**: If you're staying on the Strip, the Las Vegas Monorail is a fast and efficient way to get from one end to the other. With stops at several major hotels and attractions, it's convenient for families who want to cover more ground quickly.
- **RTC Bus System**: For areas beyond the Strip, the Regional Transportation Commission (RTC) bus system offers routes throughout the city. It's affordable and covers popular destinations like Fremont Street and the Las Vegas Arts District.

Renting a Car

For families who want to explore beyond the Strip, renting a car is a great option. This is especially helpful if you plan to visit off-the-beaten-path locations like Red Rock Canyon or the Hoover Dam. Just be aware that parking on the Strip can be expensive, so you may want to park at your hotel and walk or take public transportation to nearby attractions.

- **Parking Tips**: Many hotels on the Strip charge for parking, but some still offer free parking, especially for guests. Research ahead of time to find out which attractions offer free parking or take advantage of hotel shuttles.

Rideshare and Taxis

For quick trips across town, rideshare services like Uber and Lyft are widely available in Las Vegas. Taxis are another option, though rideshare apps tend to be more affordable and reliable.

- **Family-Friendly Rideshare**: If you're traveling with younger kids, check if your rideshare driver has a car seat or bring your own. Some rideshare services also offer family-friendly options with more space and booster seats.

Walking the Strip

Walking is one of the best ways to explore the Las Vegas Strip, with plenty of attractions located within a few blocks of each other. However, it's important to keep in mind that the distances can be deceiving due to the sheer size of the hotels and resorts. Be prepared for a lot of walking, and take breaks in between to keep your little ones from getting too tired.

- **Tip**: Take advantage of the pedestrian bridges that connect many of the hotels and casinos along the Strip. Not only are they safer than crossing the busy streets, but they also offer great views!

Safety Tips for Families

Keeping your family safe during your Las Vegas adventure is a top priority. While the city is generally family-friendly, there are a few things to keep in mind to ensure a safe and enjoyable trip.

Heat Safety

The Las Vegas desert climate can be intense, particularly during the summer. Here are some key tips to keep everyone cool and safe:

- **Stay Hydrated**: Make sure everyone in the family drinks plenty of water, even if you're not feeling thirsty. Dehydration can sneak up quickly in the desert heat.
- **Sunscreen is a Must**: Apply sunscreen every two hours, especially if you're spending time outdoors. Hats, sunglasses, and lightweight, breathable clothing can also help protect from the sun.
- **Plan for Indoor Breaks**: If you're out exploring during the hottest parts of the day (typically between 12 p.m. and 4 p.m.), make sure to schedule indoor activities like museum visits or lunch breaks to cool off.

Stay Together in Crowded Areas

Las Vegas can be crowded, especially in tourist-heavy areas like the Strip and Fremont Street. If you're visiting these spots, be sure to keep a close eye on your kids.

- **Use a Buddy System**: For older children, the buddy system can be helpful. Make sure they always stay with a sibling or parent, especially in crowded areas.
- **Set a Meeting Spot**: In case anyone gets separated, pick a designated meeting spot ahead of time. For younger kids, consider giving them a wristband with your phone number or a family contact card to carry in case they get lost.

Outdoor Safety

If your adventures take you outside the city to places like Mount Charleston or Red Rock Canyon, remember that desert environments have their own safety considerations.

- **Stick to Marked Trails**: When hiking, make sure to stay on designated trails to avoid getting lost. Trails in desert landscapes can sometimes be less defined than in other environments, so follow the markers.
- **Watch for Wildlife**: The desert is home to various wildlife, including snakes and scorpions. Teach your children to look but not touch, and always stay aware of your surroundings.

Stranger Safety

While Las Vegas is generally a safe city, it's always important to teach your children about stranger safety. Remind them to never wander off with someone they don't know and to stay close in public spaces.

- **Hotel Safety**: Many Las Vegas hotels are massive, and it's easy to get lost. Make sure your kids know your room number, or have it written down for them, in case they need help finding their way back.

Additional Information

To enhance your Las Vegas adventure, here are a few more tips and insights that will make your family's visit even more enjoyable:

Las Vegas Shows and Events

Las Vegas is famous for its live shows, and many of them are family-friendly! From Cirque du Soleil performances to magic shows and interactive theater experiences, there's something to captivate kids and adults alike.

- **Book in Advance**: Popular shows can sell out quickly, especially during peak travel times. If there's a particular show your family is excited about, be sure to book tickets in advance.
- **Matinees for Younger Kids**: If your children are younger, consider booking matinee performances. These tend to be shorter and at a time that works better for younger kids' schedules.

Special Events and Seasonal Attractions

Throughout the year, Las Vegas hosts a variety of family-friendly events and seasonal attractions. Whether it's ice skating in the winter, holiday light displays, or summer concerts in the park, there's always something happening in the city.

- **Check Local Calendars**: Before your trip, check local event calendars to see what special events are happening during your visit. Many of these events are free or low-cost and can add an extra layer of fun to your adventure.

Bringing the Fun Home

One of the best ways to remember your Las Vegas adventure is by creating a family scrapbook or photo album. Encourage your kids to save ticket stubs, brochures, and small souvenirs that can be added to the album when you get home. Not only does this extend the fun, but it also creates a lasting memory of your trip together.

With the tips and information provided in this chapter, you're well on your way to planning an unforgettable family adventure in Las Vegas! Stay safe, have fun, and enjoy all the amazing experiences that this city has to offer.

Chapter 8

Adventure Styles Overview

When planning a family trip to Las Vegas, understanding your family's adventure style is key to making the most of the experience. This chapter is designed to help you explore the various adventure styles offered in the *Mini-Adventure Planner – Las Vegas, NV-USA Edition*, so you can choose the perfect fit for your family's interests. Whether you're craving a cultural exploration or high-energy outdoor excitement, there's an adventure style for every family. Let's break down the six unique adventure styles, followed by tips on how to customize your itinerary to ensure every moment of your trip is exciting and memorable.

Choosing Your Adventure Style

1. Exploration & Discovery

If your family is driven by curiosity and loves to learn about new things, the *Exploration & Discovery* adventure style is the perfect match. This style focuses on visits to unique landmarks, hands-on exhibits, and tours of hidden gems in the city. Think of museums, walking tours, and behind-the-scenes experiences that are both educational and exciting for kids and parents alike. You can explore places that provide immersive experiences, such as fascinating museums and interactive exhibits that will captivate your kids while also sparking their curiosity.

Who It's For: Families who enjoy history, science, and hidden secrets of a city. Children aged 6 and older may get the most out of this adventure style, as they can fully participate in the activities.

Example Activities:

- Science centers with hands-on exhibits.
- Guided walking tours of historical districts.
- Behind-the-scenes tours of attractions.

2. Outdoor Adventures

Families that thrive in the great outdoors will love the *Outdoor Adventures* style. Las Vegas might be known for its glittering cityscape, but it's also a gateway to stunning natural parks, hiking trails, and adventure-filled outdoor activities. From easy family hikes to scenic picnic spots and playgrounds, this style offers a mix of physical activity and connection with nature.

Who It's For: Adventurous families who love nature and active experiences. Ideal for children aged 3 to 15, as there are options for all ability levels.

Example Activities:

- Hiking through nearby national parks.
- Visiting local playgrounds and nature reserves.
- Family-friendly rock climbing or biking.

3. Culture & Historic Adventures

Immerse your family in the cultural richness of Las Vegas through the *Culture & Historic Adventures* style. This adventure focuses on the city's history, art, and architecture. Take a deep dive into cultural festivals, art museums, and historic districts that reflect the unique blend of cultures in Las Vegas. Families will enjoy storytelling tours, performances, and visits to historic sites that make the city come alive.

Who It's For: Families who love art, history, and cultural immersion. Perfect for families with older children who can appreciate the stories behind the architecture and artistic works.

Example Activities:

- Visits to art galleries and museums.
- Cultural festivals and traditional performances.
- Touring historic neighborhoods.

4. Creativity & The Arts

For families that love to create and get hands-on with art, *Creativity & The Arts* will be your favorite adventure style. Whether it's crafting workshops, painting classes, or visits to interactive art spaces, this adventure encourages families to unleash their creativity while learning new skills. This is the ideal style for families who want to leave with not only great memories but also tangible creations from their time in the city.

Who It's For: Creative families who enjoy hands-on activities. Ideal for children aged 5 and up, particularly those who love arts and crafts.

Example Activities:

- Pottery or painting workshops.
- Family art challenges.
- Attending local art performances or theater shows.

5. The Foodie Family

For those who view food as a central part of their travel experience, *The Foodie Family* style allows families to indulge in Las Vegas's culinary offerings. From unique dining experiences to family-friendly cooking classes and food tours, this adventure style is all about discovering new flavors and culinary traditions in a fun, interactive way. Plus, there's nothing like bonding over a delicious meal at a new restaurant!

Who It's For: Families who love to explore different foods, learn about culinary traditions, and enjoy hands-on food experiences. Great for kids who are adventurous eaters or curious about cooking.

Example Activities:

- Family cooking classes.
- Food tours of local markets and restaurants.
- Visiting family-friendly restaurants with a twist.

Mike Robinson

Mike Robinson

Mike Robinson

Mike Robinson

Mike Robinson

Mike Robinson

6. Science & Education Trail

For the family that loves to learn while having fun, the *Science & Education Trail* is a fantastic option. This style focuses on educational, hands-on experiences that explore the wonders of science, technology, and the natural world. From planetarium visits to science museums, this adventure is perfect for families looking to combine fun with learning. It's the ultimate option for those who want their children to leave with new knowledge and a sense of wonder.

Who It's For: Families with children aged 5 and up who love science, discovery, and interactive learning.

Example Activities:

- Science museum visits.
- Interactive planetarium shows.
- Discovery tours focusing on wildlife or the environment.

Customizing Your Itinerary

Now that you've identified the adventure styles that most appeal to your family, it's time to think about how you can customize your itinerary to fit your schedule, interests, and energy levels. Here are some tips to make the most of your trip, no matter which adventure style you choose:

1. Mix and Match Adventures

Don't feel like you need to stick to just one adventure style! Las Vegas offers a diverse range of activities, so you can easily mix a morning outdoor hike with an afternoon at a museum or art gallery. Keep your family's interests in mind, but also try adding a surprise activity from a different style to broaden the experience.

Example:

- Combine a Science & Education morning at a local planetarium with a Creativity & The Arts afternoon by attending a painting workshop.
- Spend a morning hiking a family-friendly trail (Outdoor Adventures), then enjoy a family food tour in the afternoon (The Foodie Family).

2. Adjust Based on Energy Levels

Children (and adults) have varying energy levels throughout the day, so plan accordingly. If your family tends to be more energetic in the morning, consider scheduling high-energy activities like hiking or exploring. Save quieter, more educational experiences for the afternoon when everyone might appreciate a slower pace.

3. Allow Flexibility in Your Itinerary

It's important to leave room for spontaneity in your plans. While it's helpful to have a structured itinerary, allow some time for unplanned discoveries—whether it's stumbling upon a local café or deciding to spend an extra hour at an art gallery that captures your child's interest.

4. Use Travel Tools

Don't forget to utilize travel tools like mobile apps for maps, food tours, or museum exhibit guides to enhance your experience. These tools can help your family stay organized and make the most of your time in the city.

Useful Travel Apps:

- Google Maps: For navigation and finding points of interest.
- TripAdvisor: To read reviews and find hidden gems.
- Specific museum or attraction apps that provide additional information or augmented reality features.

Mike Robinson

5. Personalize the Adventure

Consider what excites your family the most and tailor your trip accordingly. For example, if your child is fascinated by space, center your day around visiting the local planetarium and following it up with a space-themed exhibit or a documentary screening.

By customizing your itinerary to match your family's preferences, you'll ensure that every adventure is personal and memorable.

With these adventure styles and customization tips in hand, you're ready to create a family adventure that's as unique as your family! Whether you choose to explore the city's cultural treasures or its thrilling outdoor experiences, you're guaranteed to find something for everyone. Enjoy your Las Vegas adventure, and remember that the best memories come from the adventures that suit your family's unique style!

Chapter 9

Extra Places Worth Checking Out

Las Vegas is much more than the glittering Strip and famous landmarks. For families looking to uncover something beyond the usual tourist spots, this chapter offers hidden gems and unique experiences that are well worth checking out. Whether you're looking for an off-the-beaten-path adventure or a special place that didn't make it into previous chapters, this list will give your family even more to explore. From quirky attractions to serene spots, these locations provide a fresh perspective on a city that's constantly evolving. Let's dive into some of the lesser-known places and fascinating highlights of Las Vegas.

---

1. Pinball Hall of Fame

A throwback to an earlier era, the Pinball Hall of Fame is a delightful, interactive museum filled with pinball machines dating from the 1950s to today. This place offers a hands-on history lesson for kids and adults alike, as everyone can try their hand at these vintage machines. With rows upon rows of flashing lights and sound effects, it's a nostalgic escape from the modern world, and kids will love the chance to play these mechanical wonders.

Fun Fact: The Pinball Hall of Fame operates as a nonprofit, and all excess revenues go to charity! It's entertainment that gives back to the community.

Address: 4925 S Las Vegas Blvd, Las Vegas, NV 89119
Website: pinballmuseum.org
Operating Hours: Open daily from 11 AM to 9 PM.

2. The Ethel M Chocolate Factory and Botanical Cactus Garden

For families with a sweet tooth, a visit to the Ethel M Chocolate Factory in nearby Henderson is a must. Take a self-guided tour of the chocolate-making process and indulge in free samples along the way. But the real surprise is the adjacent Botanical Cactus Garden, home to over 300 species of desert plants. This serene desert garden offers a nice balance of education and nature appreciation, giving families a peaceful space to explore and learn about unique desert flora.

Pro Tip: Visit during the holiday season to see the garden decked out in colorful lights, turning it into a winter wonderland.

Address: 2 Cactus Garden Dr, Henderson, NV 89014
Website: ethelm.com
Operating Hours: Open daily from 10 AM to 6 PM.

3. Seven Magic Mountains

If your family loves art, you won't want to miss Seven Magic Mountains, a colorful and surreal art installation located just outside the city. Created by Swiss artist Ugo Rondinone, this public art piece features seven towering stacks of brightly painted boulders set against the stark desert landscape. It's a stunning sight that blends nature and art in a way that will captivate children and adults alike.

Did You Know? Each boulder weighs up to 25 tons, and the entire installation is about 35 feet high! It's an Instagram favorite, so be sure to bring a camera.

Address: S Las Vegas Blvd, Las Vegas, NV 89054
Website: sevenmagicmountains.com
Operating Hours: Open 24 hours a day, free to the public.

4. Zak Bagans' The Haunted Museum

For families with older children who enjoy a thrill, Zak Bagans' The Haunted Museum offers an eerie and fascinating look at haunted artifacts, paranormal history, and macabre curiosities. It's a spooky adventure that mixes history with a bit of supernatural flair. The museum is filled with haunted objects from across the world, and each exhibit comes with a chilling backstory.

Important Note: While this museum is best suited for families with teenagers, it's not recommended for young children due to its creepy atmosphere.

Address: 600 E Charleston Blvd, Las Vegas, NV 89104
Website: thehauntedmuseum.com
Operating Hours: Open daily, check website for tour times.

5. Springs Preserve's Hidden Trails

Though the Springs Preserve was likely covered in other chapters, many families overlook its beautiful hidden trails. Tucked away from the main exhibits, these scenic trails wind through desert landscapes and offer quiet spots for reflection and wildlife watching. The trails are easy to navigate and perfect for younger children, offering educational markers about local plant life along the way. It's a serene getaway just minutes from downtown.

Insider Tip: Don't forget to pack water and wear sunscreen—these trails can get hot, especially during midday.

Address: 333 S Valley View Blvd, Las Vegas, NV 89107
Website: springspreserve.org
Operating Hours: Open daily from 9 AM to 5 PM.

---

6. Gilcrease Orchard

Yes, you can visit a working orchard right in Las Vegas! Gilcrease Orchard is a hidden gem where families can pick their own fresh produce, including apples, pears, and pumpkins, depending on the season. It's a wonderful way to teach kids about where food comes from while enjoying the outdoors. The orchard also has a small store offering fresh apple cider and other treats made from their own produce.

Best Time to Visit: Fall is the perfect time to visit the orchard for pumpkin picking and hayrides.

Address: 7800 N Tenaya Way, Las Vegas, NV 89131
Website: thegilcreaseorchard.org
Operating Hours: Check the website for seasonal hours.

7. Las Vegas Springs Tower

Few people know about the Las Vegas Springs Tower, a viewing platform located within Springs Preserve that offers panoramic views of the Las Vegas Valley. The tower provides families with a unique vantage point to take in the natural beauty of the surrounding desert as well as the distant cityscape. It's a perfect spot for a family photo or simply to admire the views and take a break from the day's adventures.

Quick Tip: Visit at sunset for the best lighting and a truly breathtaking view.

8. Nevada State Railroad Museum in Boulder City

Located just a short drive from Las Vegas, the Nevada State Railroad Museum is a delightful place for families to explore the rich history of railroads in the state. The museum features restored locomotives, passenger cars, and even offers train rides on certain weekends. It's a hit with kids who love trains and offers a fun, educational experience outside the city.

Bonus Experience: If your visit falls on the right weekend, you can hop aboard a historic train for a short ride through the desert landscape.

Address: 601 Yucca St, Boulder City, NV 89005
Website: nevadasouthern.com
Operating Hours: Check the website for hours and train schedules.

9. The Old Las Vegas Mormon Fort

For a historical experience, visit the Old Las Vegas Mormon Fort, the first permanent structure built in the Las Vegas Valley. This reconstructed fort tells the story of early settlers in Nevada and offers interactive displays that bring history to life for children. The fort is located within a state park, providing both a history lesson and a chance to enjoy the outdoors.

Did You Know? The fort was originally established in 1855 by Mormon missionaries and played a significant role in the early development of the region.

Address: 500 E Washington Ave, Las Vegas, NV 89101
Website: https://parks.nv.gov/parks/old-las-vegas-mormon-fort
Operating Hours: Open daily from 8 AM to 4:30 PM.

As you can see, there's a lot more to Las Vegas than meets the eye. From nature escapes and quirky museums to historic landmarks and serene orchards, this city offers a range of experiences that cater to curious kids and adventurous parents. Whether you're looking for educational stops or simply want to add a little variety to your trip, these extra places are sure to make your family's adventure even more memorable. Make sure to add a few of these hidden gems to your itinerary for a well-rounded, unforgettable Las Vegas experience!

Chapter 10

Resources & Additional Information

This chapter compiles all the helpful resources and additional information referenced throughout the **Mini-Adventure Planner – Las Vegas, NV-USA Edition**. Whether you're looking for contact details, helpful tools, or other valuable information, this section provides a convenient summary to ensure your Las Vegas family adventure is as smooth and enjoyable as possible. We've organized everything into categories to make it easy to navigate.

Museums and Cultural Centers

1. **Las Vegas Natural History Museum**
    Address: 900 Las Vegas Blvd N, Las Vegas, NV 89101
    Phone: (702) 384-3466
    Website: lvnhm.org
    Operating Hours: Open daily from 9 AM to 4 PM
    Details: Explore exhibits that delve into Nevada's natural history, world cultures, and prehistoric life. Ideal for children aged 3 and up.

2. **The Mob Museum**
   Address: 300 Stewart Ave, Las Vegas, NV 89101
   Phone: (702) 229-2734
   Website: themobmuseum.org
   Operating Hours: Open daily from 9 AM to 9 PM
   Details: Learn about the history of organized crime in the United
   States through interactive exhibits and storytelling.

3. **Discovery Children's Museum**
   Address: 360 Promenade Place, Las Vegas, NV 89106
   Phone: (702) 382-3445
   Website: discoverykidslv.org
   Operating Hours: Open Tuesday to Sunday, from 10 AM to 5 PM
   Details: A fun, hands-on environment where kids can learn through
   play. Great for families with younger children.

Outdoor Adventures & Parks

1. **Red Rock Canyon National Conservation Area**
   Address: 1000 Scenic Loop Dr, Las Vegas, NV 89161
   Phone: (702) 515-5350
   Website: redrockcanyonlv.org
   Operating Hours: Visitor Center open daily from 8 AM to 4:30 PM
   Details: Ideal for families who love outdoor activities like hiking and rock climbing. Explore scenic trails and the beauty of the Mojave Desert.

2. **Clark County Wetlands Park**
   Address: 7050 Wetlands Park Ln, Las Vegas, NV 89122
   Phone: (702) 455-7522
   Website: clarkcountynv.gov
   Operating Hours: Park open from dawn to dusk, Nature Center open from 9 AM to 3 PM daily
   Details: An expansive park perfect for birdwatching, nature walks, and learning about Nevada's ecosystem.

Art & Creativity Hotspots

1. **Seven Magic Mountains**
   Location: S Las Vegas Blvd, Las Vegas, NV 89054
   Website: sevenmagicmountains.com
   Details: A public art installation by Swiss artist Ugo Rondinone, featuring brightly colored boulders stacked in the middle of the desert. Free to visit, and ideal for a creative family outing.

2. **The Neon Museum**
   Address: 770 Las Vegas Blvd N, Las Vegas, NV 89101
   Phone: (702) 387-6366
   Website: neonmuseum.org
   Operating Hours: Open daily from 9 AM to 7 PM
   Details: This museum preserves iconic Las Vegas signage and is a great way to learn about the city's vibrant history through its neon lights.

Food & Dining Options

1. **Ethel M Chocolate Factory and Botanical Cactus Garden**
   Address: 2 Cactus Garden Dr, Henderson, NV 89014
   Phone: (702) 435-2608
   Website: ethelm.com
   Details: Enjoy self-guided tours of the chocolate factory and explore the adjacent botanical garden, filled with unique desert plants. Free samples included!

2. **Black Tap Craft Burgers & Beer**
Address: 3355 Las Vegas Blvd S, Las Vegas, NV 89109
Phone: (702) 795-8000
Website: blacktap.com
Details: A fun and casual dining experience with specialty burgers and their famous CrazyShakes, perfect for kids and parents alike.

Educational Tools & Resources

1. **Google Maps**
Website: maps.google.com
Details: Use Google Maps for navigating Las Vegas, discovering new attractions, and planning daily itineraries. It's great for figuring out the best routes to various destinations.

2. **Springs Preserve Educational Tools**
Website: springspreserve.org
Details: Offers educational materials for families, including nature guides, local history, and scientific resources to enhance your visit.

3. **Clark County Wetlands Park Educational Tools**
Website: clarkcountynv.gov
Details: Offers resources for understanding local wildlife, ecosystems, and conservation efforts. Perfect for homeschooling families or those looking to dive deeper into the natural side of Nevada.

Adventure & Exploration Apps

1. **Roadtrippers**
   Website: roadtrippers.com
   Details: An excellent app for families planning a road trip around Las Vegas or beyond. Customize your route to include scenic byways, quirky roadside attractions, and family-friendly stops.

2. **AllTrails**
   Website: alltrails.com
   Details: Great for finding hiking trails in and around Las Vegas. AllTrails offers user reviews, difficulty ratings, and GPS navigation for outdoor enthusiasts.

Transport & Navigating the City

1. **Las Vegas Monorail**
   Website: lvmonorail.com
   Details: A convenient way for families to get around the Strip without the hassle of driving. Perfect for quick trips between casinos and attractions, offering daily passes for unlimited rides.

2. **RTC Southern Nevada (Bus Service)**
   Website: rtcsnv.com
   Details: The Regional Transportation Commission operates the public bus system in Las Vegas. Affordable and reliable, it's a good option for getting around the city.

Safety Tips and Considerations

- **Hydration is Key:** Las Vegas is in the middle of the desert, so families should be prepared for hot, dry conditions, especially in the summer. Always carry water with you and remind kids to hydrate frequently.
- **Sun Protection:** Whether you're exploring the Neon Boneyard or hiking in Red Rock Canyon, sunscreen, hats, and sunglasses are a must to protect against the strong Nevada sun.
- **Stick Together:** With so many attractions and crowded spots, it's easy for families to get separated. Make sure everyone knows a meeting spot, and for younger children, consider using child safety wristbands with contact details.

Hidden Gems & Local Secrets

1. **Gilcrease Orchard**
   Address: 7800 N Tenaya Way, Las Vegas, NV 89131
   Phone: (702) 409-0655
   Website: thegilcreaseorchard.org
   Details: This pick-your-own orchard offers seasonal fruits and vegetables. It's a lovely place for families to spend time outdoors while learning about local agriculture.

2. **Old Las Vegas Mormon Fort State Historic Park**
   Address: 500 E Washington Ave, Las Vegas, NV 89101
   Phone: (702) 486-3511
   Website: https://parks.nv.gov/parks/old-las-vegas-mormon-fort
   Details: Step back in time to explore the oldest building in Las Vegas and learn about the area's early settlers. It's a quiet spot away from the crowds, offering a blend of history and culture.

Final Travel Tips

- **Time Your Visits:** Las Vegas is bustling during peak tourist seasons, so plan accordingly. Early mornings and weekdays are less crowded for popular attractions like the Neon Museum or Red Rock Canyon.
- **Plan for Breaks:** The heat and excitement of Las Vegas can be overwhelming for little ones. Schedule in some downtime, whether that's a break at a family-friendly café or a relaxing afternoon at your hotel's pool.
- **Mix It Up:** Las Vegas offers a wide variety of experiences, from outdoor adventures to indoor educational exhibits. Mix up your days so kids don't get bored, and parents get a break from the high-energy activities.

This comprehensive guide aims to enhance your family's visit by providing all the essential information in one place. With these resources, your Las Vegas adventure will be a breeze—ensuring your trip is both exciting and well-organized!

Chapter 11

Wrapping Up This Adventure

As you reach the end of this **Mini-Adventure Planner – Las Vegas, NV-USA Edition**, your family's journey through one of the most dynamic cities in the world is just beginning. Las Vegas is so much more than its bright lights and bustling casinos. It is a place rich in culture, history, and natural beauty that offers endless opportunities for exploration. Whether you've visited only a few of the highlighted locations or experienced them all, there's always something new to discover.

Encouraging Continued Exploration

We hope this planner has sparked a love for adventure in your family, but remember, Las Vegas is always changing, evolving, and expanding. Beyond the pages of this guide, there are countless neighborhoods, hidden gems, and seasonal events that await your family's discovery. Make time to explore those lesser-known parks, local food spots, or art installations scattered around the city. Perhaps you'll discover a family favorite that wasn't in the book!

Las Vegas is unique in its ability to offer something for every type of adventurer. Whether you're drawn to the beauty of the desert landscapes, fascinated by its rich history, or excited about its cutting-edge entertainment and technology, there are always new stories to create and memories to capture. Take this as an invitation to return to Las Vegas again and again — each visit offering a fresh perspective and a new chapter to your family's adventure story.

Don't let your exploration stop at the city limits. Las Vegas is also the perfect launchpad for day trips and excursions into nearby areas like Hoover Dam, Lake Mead, or the scenic beauty of the Valley of Fire. Adventure knows no boundaries, and neither should your curiosity!

Staying Connected and Sharing Experiences

One of the most rewarding aspects of travel is sharing your adventures with others. Whether it's through stories around the dinner table, photo albums, or social media, capturing and sharing these moments is a way to keep the spirit of adventure alive long after your trip ends. We encourage your family to stay connected with the larger community of explorers by sharing your Las Vegas experiences online.

Join fellow families by using hashtags like **#VegasFamilyAdventures** or **#MiniAdventuresLV** to post about your favorite spots, recommendations, and unforgettable moments. Sharing your story can inspire others to explore Las Vegas with the same enthusiasm and curiosity. You can also connect with travel communities on platforms like Facebook, Instagram, or dedicated travel blogs where you'll find tips and new ideas for your next family trip.

In addition to social media, consider keeping a family travel journal. Encourage each family member, from the youngest to the oldest, to write or draw something special from each day of your Las Vegas adventure. This not only helps to cement those cherished memories but also provides a creative outlet for everyone to reflect on the trip.

Your feedback is invaluable as well. Let us know how you enjoyed the adventures in this planner! Join online discussions, leave reviews for family-friendly places you visited, and share your insights with others who are planning their own Vegas family adventure. Together, we can make family travel even more exciting and inclusive.

Final Words

As you wrap up your Las Vegas adventure, we hope this guide has provided your family with more than just a travel itinerary. We hope it has encouraged curiosity, sparked creativity, and created lasting memories that your children will cherish for years to come. Adventure is not just about the places you visit, but the experiences you share, the lessons you learn, and the bonds you strengthen as a family.

Las Vegas will always have something new waiting for you. Until your next adventure, keep exploring, keep discovering, and most importantly, keep making memories together. Safe travels, and we hope to see you back in the city of endless possibilities soon!

About the Author

Mike Robinson is a passionate explorer, storyteller, and lover of all things adventure. With a keen eye for discovering hidden gems and crafting family-friendly experiences, Mike has spent over a decade sharing his love for travel and local exploration through writing. His aim is to inspire families to go beyond the obvious and immerse themselves in the unique culture and history of each place they visit.

As a father, Mike understands the importance of making travel fun, active, entertaining, and educational for children. He combines his experiences as a parent with his expertise in storytelling to create guides that cater to both the young and the young at heart. Whether it's offering tips on family-friendly dining, uncovering hands-on educational activities, or designing itineraries that make every family trip unforgettable, Mike's goal is to turn every journey into an adventure for all ages.

When he's not writing or exploring new destinations, you can find Mike at home with his family, planning their next big adventure. His motto? "Adventure is everywhere—you just have to know where to look."

Acknowledgments

I would like to extend my deepest gratitude to my wonderful kids, whose unwavering love and support have been my greatest source of inspiration. To my family and friends, thank you for always believing in me, encouraging me to pursue my dreams, and standing by my side through every challenge. Your encouragement has meant the world to me, and I am truly grateful.

To my readers, I offer my heartfelt thanks. Your time, interest, and support are invaluable, and I am deeply honored that you have chosen to engage with my work. I hope it resonates with you as much as it has with me, and I am endlessly appreciative of your role in this journey.

Made in the USA
Coppell, TX
20 December 2024

43287576R00066